SAVING WHISKEY

SAVING WHISKEY

A Holistic Journey of Discovery and Healing

TRACIE MERCURI

www.sunflowerlove.com.au

Copyright © 2023 by Tracie Mercuri

This book contains a true account of events. The ideas, suggestions and procedures provided are not intended as a substitute for seeking medical advice.

All rights reserved. No part of this book may be reproduced in any manner whatsoever without written permission except in the case of brief quotations embodied in critical articles and reviews.

First Printing, 2023

Published by Sunflower Love
www.sunflowerlove.com.au

CONTENTS

PREFACE vii

1 WHISKEY 1
2 INFLUENCES 4
3 METHOD 6
4 RESULTS 14
5 SUMMATION 17

GLOSSARY 19
NOTES 21
About The Author 22

PREFACE

Saving Whiskey is the true account of what happened when the combination of a lifelong love of horses, a passion for Complementary Health and Energetic Medicine got caught up with a chronic case of curiosity.

In 2000, for reasons that will be explained in another writing, I embarked on a journey into the world of Kinesiology - the method of Biofeedback through muscle testing. My intention at the time was to assist my family as they had received encouraging, well realistically transformational results from this practice and the Practitioner had moved overseas leaving a huge hole in my ability to care for my family.

Living in a small traditional rural community word travels quickly when someone has stepped out of the "ordinary" but being part of a generational local family, people were curious and wanted to give this muscle testing thing a go.

2001, my Kinesiology Practice exploded. People travelled from all over the district, neighbouring districts and from interstate. Quite overwhelming given they couldn't even pronounce the word Kinesiology let alone explain what they had just experienced. All they knew was that it worked! It was around this time I had called an Equine Chiropractor, Steve Webb. Steve is still very well known in our area and I needed his help with a grey gelding that I owned. As he worked on the grey he would chat in between adjustments, asking what I did professionally. I told him I was a Kinesiologist. Fully expecting the usual response of " You're a What? What on earth is that?" I got, " Great! You know you can do that on the horses?!" That comment was all I needed and working on horses or animals is one of the most exciting practices I do, time permitting.

I was introduced to the art of Dowsing in 2005. It changed the way I could work in unimaginable ways and to this day it still surprises and delights me. It was the beginning of 2006 when Whiskey arrived at my property. A journey in retrospect that fills me with wonder and faith that anything is possible.

CHAPTER 1

WHISKEY

Narrandera Pony Club Camp 1998, I'd been invited to attend as a guest instructor. I was so excited, I love watching the partnerships between horse and rider grow. It's a wonderful experience, with lifelong memories and bonds being formed.

My first troop for the day included a 9yr old boy named Lochlan who was getting frustrated with his very smart looking Palomino Pony. The morning session was flat work which bores young riders as they are more geared to the " fast fun stuff". However, by the end of the flat work session the troop had gained more control of their ponies and were looking forward to the morning tea break. It was over a cuppa that Lochlan's mother Linda, explained that the Palomino Pony was a new acquisition and her son had only just started riding him. A 6yr old green broke gelding named Whiskey. Very quiet and clearly had a thing or three to teach a young rider. Linda had all 5 of her children participating at the camp and checked in with each instructor at the end of every session. The week-long camp always provided the children with a confidence boost that always translated into huge improvements for horse and young riders.

Fast forward to August 2005. Linda, Lochlan's mum purchased the property next door to ours. Their moving process is something we still joke about as the day the "Clampetts' ' moved to town. Five kids, five horses, five dogs and one cat! The family definitely loved their animals and settled into the neighbourhood enjoying everything it had to offer.

Linda was aware of my Kinesiology Practice and my history working on people and horses. She was absolutely fascinated by the biofeedback process, so much so that I'd worked on one of her horses a couple of years prior and basically turned into their horses "preventative care practitioner".

December 2005 having a chat over the fence while her farrier was shoeing and trimming horses. Linda was talking about a call she had received the previous evening from a friend who had purchased one of her ponies. The horse had a growth on the underside of his sheath. Two biopsies three months apart resulted in a cancer diagnosis with the vet advising the pony should be put down, and if Linda and the children would like to come and say their goodbyes before the scheduled euthanizing. The farrier suggested it sounded more like Habronema Worm and a specific drench often sorted the problem. Ray was an exceptional farrier and an even handier horseman who's attitude was It doesn't matter what they say, it's what you say and what you're prepared to do!

Linda called me the next day and asked if I had time for a cuppa as there was something she wanted to run past me.

We spoke about how difficult good safe kids ponies were to find and that she had convinced the pony's owner to give him some more time if I would agree to work with him.

How hard could it be? Habronema Worm, appropriate drench and test what other protocols that may assist, school holidays, nothing to lose by having a look. I had no clue as to what was to come.

Whiskey arrived at our Nallabooma property on the 14th January 2006, looking in very good condition given his diagnosis. It was agreed he would stay with me till we had a result one way or the other. The owner agreed to provide his feed for the duration of his stay

CHAPTER 2

INFLUENCES

I was at that time working with and learning from Jeptha Gates. An American Integrative Biological Agriculturalist who used Radionic Diagnostics and Dowsing to develop remedies for soil health. Jep was passionate about soil health which directly impacted plant, animal and human health.

His work changed what was possible in my mind and he and his wife Zada showed me a unique form of dowsing which assisted in determining which vitamin or mineral could assist animal or human health. They also introduced me to the world of Homoeopathic Medicine, my mind was opening to the endless possibilities and how what I was learning could be integrated into my Practice.

In the very early days of my practice I met Lloyd Charles, a local BioDynamic Farmer who became a trusted friend and a constant source of information. A brilliant researcher who can unearth information and drip feed my ever expanding mind and Practice. He would patiently repeat information I didn't understand or absorb the first, second, third or tenth time. A role he still plays to this very day.

In 2005 Lloyd was working in the US and sought out a fellow by the name of Raymon Grace. He spent a considerable amount of time with Raymon, learning his dowsing techniques. Raymon, not being one to travel, gave Lloyd his blessing to teach his techniques in Australia. These protocols were in my clinic for quite a while before I picked them up and used them the way I do today.

Working with Whiskey was the beginning of my Dowsing and Homeopathics Modality.

And So It Begins.

CHAPTER 3

METHOD

15th January 2006 work began on Whiskey. What follows is the Homoeopathic and Dowsing Processes used.
WARNING
Graphic images.
9.30am Homeopathics Pulsatilla
Causticum > Infused into
Ruta > Kidney
Secale
5mls ProBiotic (Jep Gates Gut Ruminant Formulation) given Orally.
Silicea
Gumbi Seed Pod > infused into navel.
Sabina
Ignatia
Spigelia > 3 pillules of each given orally.
Cocculus
3pm Dowsing: parasites/worms in kidney

Frozen muscles Kidney Meridian
Homeopathics: Lac can
Rumex > infused Kidney
Spigelia
Rumimate > infused Large Intestine
4mls ProBiotic orally
7pm Homeopathics: Natrum Mur
Gumbi Seed Pod > infused
Nat Sulph
Sulphur x 5 pillules
Thuja x 5 pillules > Orally
4mls ProBiotic
16th January 2006
8.30am Dowsing : Tribal beliefs
Homeopathics : Chamomilla
Pyrogenium > infused into Heart Meridian
Merc V
Kali Bi
Ruta > infused into Heart Meridian
Gumbi seed pod
Pyrogenium x 5 pillules
Symphytum x 5 pillules > orally
Cuprum x 5 pillules
4 mls Pro Biotic
Dowsed 7 hours till next check.
5.17pm
Dowsing: Whiskey's life force energy 97%
Worm life force energy active? Yes
Worm life force 63%

Does the parasite have a spirit? yes
Does the parasite have reproductive intelligence? Yes
N E F's ? yes
Raymon Grace : Scramble the frequency of/ deactivate/ re-allocate.
Infused appropriate frequency.
Infused vibrational frequency of No 60
Infused homoeopathic Thuja.
Applied purple spray and ProBiotic.
Retest: N E F's ? no
Parasite life force energy? 12%
Whiskey's life force energy? 190
Parasite reproductive intelligence? no
Parasite has a spirit? no
Also checked for negative and low level entities. No to both
Emotion > Disappointment >> adjusted
No hands on work required at this time, next check in @ 8.45pm.
8.45pm: Parasitical life force? 9%
Corrected through Grace Protocol
Parasitical life force 0%
10 mls Probiotic > orally
17th January 2006 9am
Spinal reflex > kidney
" " > large intestine
Homoeopathic > Thuja orally
Probiotic > applied to tumour

It was at this point in the process when Linda and I were standing approximately 4 metres away from Whiskey as I was using dowsing rods to scramble life force, spirit and reproductive intelligence of parasites. Whiskey was finishing off his morning feed, head down and his rump facing us which was my focus point. Two separate streams of a "steamy mist" were rising up from the middle of the left rump and the second was rising from the left hip area. Not quite believing what I was witnessing I said to Linda " Are you seeing what I'm seeing?" She said "if it's the two streams of mist coming from the left rump hip area, then yes I am!"

Life force, spirit and reproductive intelligence of parasite 0%

Next check is 8 hrs

5.30pm: Pulsatilla, Merc V, China O, infused into neuro emotional points.

Thuja infused into spinal reflex.

Ruminate infused into Large Intestine.

Minerals infused to boost physical energy

Next check 25 hours.

18th January 2006 6.30pm

Observation: Tumour starting to come away, near side travelling clockwise when facing horses head. Separation occurring around the circumference of the tumour, appears to be a third of the way around at this time.

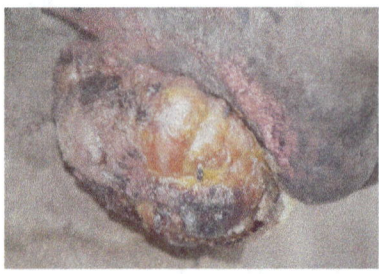

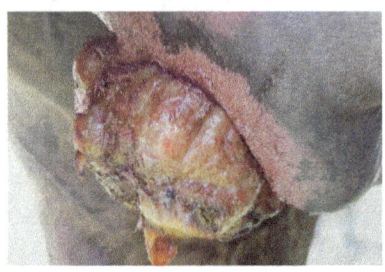

Frozen muscle > spleen
Pulsatilla, Thuja > orally
Neuro Emotional point for spleen stimulated.

As the tumour is detaching/letting go from the outer part of the sheath, so are the causal emotions.> Affectionate > too scared to get attached because they outgrow him. Never gets to stay.

Homoeopathic > Kali Phos infused.

Next check 2 days.

20th January 2006 5pm

Homeopathics: Rumex, Thuja & Urtica administered orally.

8.30pm

Homeopathics: Kali Carb, China O administered orally.

21st January 2006 5.30am

Homeopathics: Thuja, Nux V, Cimicifuga administered orally

Spigelia infused into spleen
The emotion coming up at this time > Defeated.
2pm
Homeopathic: Pulsatilla infused.
8pm
Homeopathics: Pulsatilla infused.
22nd January 2006 8am
Homeopathics: Thuja, Digitalis infused
Purple Spray > applied
12 noon.
Homeopathic Kali Carb orally
5pm
Frozen muscles > adjust manually
Emotions affecting pathology > stomach and kidney.
Indifference and Disconnection.

We are losing him, we need to provide a purpose. We dowsed Whiskey's preferred rider for some gentle exercise

hoping this would show him we were listening and that he had a choice.

My eldest daughter Tess is his preferred jockey. Fingers crossed!!

25th January 2006.
7am: Homeopathics Chamomilla
Thuja > Administered 3 x day
Pyrogenium @ 7am, 12 noon, 5pm
Rumimate 6mls for the next 5 days.
30th January 2006.
7am: Homeopathics China O
Podophyllum > Infused
5pm: Homeopathics Euphrasia
Ignatia > Administered

This was the last of the homeopathics, dowsing and physical work Whiskey required. It was a case of wait and watch.

The tumour was an upside down iceberg. What was visible was only a fraction of what was hidden internally. As the tumour descended I was convinced it would drop out in its entirety. So convinced, we went on observation vigils, morning and evening feeds were full of anticipation.

Would today be the day we would find the tumour on the ground?

Over the coming weeks the tumour descended and ruptured, descended and ruptured. Whiskey was happy enough and enjoyed the gentle exercise Tess was giving him but we certainly didn't feel we were in for a positive outcome.

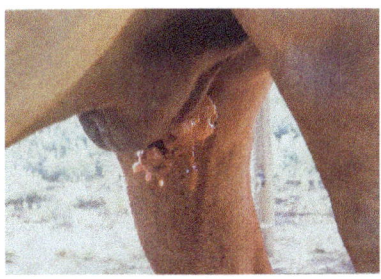

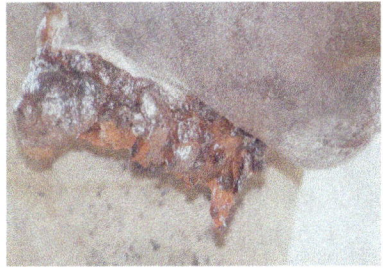

CHAPTER 4

RESULTS

16 weeks into our Whiskey journey, I headed down to do the morning feeds and was met with a sight that looked a little like a massacre!

Whiskey's hind legs were blood stained as was his tail, I rang Linda who jumped the fence and immediately started to search his day yard looking for pieces of the tumour. Nothing! It wasn't until I haltered the Palomino Pony that I realised his muzzle was also blood stained, then the enormity of what had happened hit us.

Whiskey had chewed it off!

The smell of that tumour was like nothing I've ever smelt before or since.

A smell that lingered and one I'll never forget. It was the smell of death!

The smell disappeared that day.

How did Whiskey know when the time was right to rid himself of the tumour?

How did he know to chew it off?
Natural Instinct!
Amazing!!
Every day he chewed more and more until there was nothing left. The final scar being no bigger than my thumb nail.

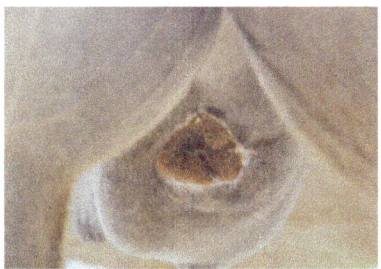

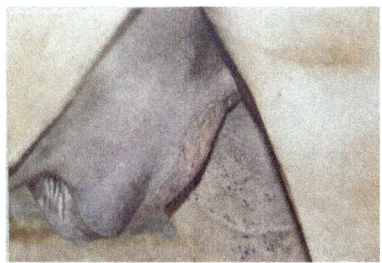

Whiskey's owners left him with us as we were better equipped to work with him should the tumour return and Tess was happy to have him as her pony. Given our unique understanding of his emotional "point of view", that being he couldn't get close to his riders as they always outgrew him and then he was moved on.

This aspect of Whiskey was always uppermost in my mind and I was determined to do the right thing by the pony.

When the time came for Whiskey to be moved on he was given to a local horsey family with property at Morundah. He spent the rest of his days at Morundah with the odd 6 month stint to get a beginner rider up and going, but then straight back to the farm. He spent his life living on the creek with a herd of horses, he was used for mustering and pleasure rides.

Whiskey passed away of natural causes in 2020 at the age of 28. The Tumour never returned, he remained healthy and robust till the end.

CHAPTER 5

SUMMATION

The synchronicities of Whiskey's story are not lost on me. I still marvel at the people who turned up at exactly the right time, with exactly the right expertise or exactly the right information. Whiskey certainly taught us a thing or two about what is possible.

Energy Medicine is one of the most powerful, underrated modalities. I believe it will be used by many as they begin to understand their energetic environment, the power they have to heal themselves, and potentially others, if they choose.

"If you ever doubt what you can do. Just remember that Palomino Pony" Lloyd Charles

"If you do nothing, nothing will happen, If you do something, something might happen, The Future Is Yours, Do Something About It!" Raymon Grace

"It's amazing what you can do when you don't know you can't". Raymon Grace

GLOSSARY

- **BIO FEEDBACK-** A type of mind-body technique you use to control some of your body's functions, such as your heart rate, breathing patterns and muscle responses
- **DOWSING** - (Water Witching, Divining, Questing, Doodlebugging...) is the ancient art of finding water, minerals and other objects that seem to have a natural magnetic, electromagnetic or other perhaps unknown energy. Energies that the body seems to detect with its built-in, laboratory demonstrable sensors, that are no more mysterious than seeing, hearing or feeling, and seem to be natural to all of us. As it is with music, many persons can develop a degree of dowsing skill with training and practice.
- **ENERGY MEDICINE** - Any energetic or informational interaction with a biological system to bring back homeostasis in the organism
- **GREEN BROKE-** Refers to a horse that's newly started under the saddle
- **HABRONEMA WORM-**Equine stomach worms that can cause tumour like swellings

- **HOMEOPATHY** - A medical system based on the belief that the body can cure itself
- **THE MERCURI METHOD** - A home based practice of biofeedback developed by the author. It uses dowsing to assist one to determine what may be causing interference within the physical, mental, emotional or energetic body.

NOTES

Tracie Mercuri is a wife, mother, entrepreneur, guest speaker and teacher of The Mercuri Method. Tracie has 23 years experience working in her Kinesiology clinic in rural NSW, Australia. She is known as the Energetic GP and attracts clients from all over the country.

This first time author is sharing uplifting true accounts of positive health outcomes using her alternative methods.

www.ingramcontent.com/pod-product-compliance
Lightning Source LLC
Chambersburg PA
CBHW070714020526
44107CB00078B/2577